Khan

by Iain Gray

79 Main Street, Newtongrange,
Midlothian EH22 4NA
Tel: 0131 344 0414   Fax: 0845 075 6085
E-mail: info@lang-syne.co.uk
www.langsyneshop.co.uk

Design by Dorothy Meikle
Printed by Blissetts
© Lang Syne Publishers Ltd 2021

All rights reserved. No part of this publication may be reproduced, stored or introduced into a retrieval system, or transmitted in any form or by any means (electronic, mechanical, photocopying, recording or otherwise) without the prior written permission of Lang Syne Publishers Ltd.

ISBN 978-1-85217-783-6

Chapter one:
Origins of names from the Indian subcontinent

by Iain Gray

With a population of more than one billion souls, India is the second most populated country in the world, while Pakistan, with more than 182 million, is ranked sixth and Bangladesh fifth.

Part of the vast Indian subcontinent, India is a nation that is home to a rich mix of ethnic groups, religions and cultures – and this is reflected on a truly dramatic scale through the immense variety of family names and naming conventions.

These are names found today not only in India itself, but also scattered throughout the world as many Indians, in common with the Scots and the Irish of earlier generations, sought fresh opportunities for themselves and their kinsfolk in foreign lands.

This, in turn, has not only added to the cultural diversity of those nations in which they settled and in which their descendants now thrive, but has also seen the importation to the West of what were previously wholly 'foreign' names.

These are commonly found in telephone directories throughout the world today, but to trace their origins we have to travel back through the dim mists of time to the great sub-continent of India itself – a vast landmass which from earliest times was home to a highly sophisticated civilisation.

The naming conventions and styles are as complex – often bewilderingly so – as they are varied, with significant differences occurring.

These are not only among the nation's states, or regions, such as Gujarat, West Bengal, Bihar, Jharkhand, Orissa, Andhra Pradesh, Himachal Pradesh, Rajasthan, Uttarakhand, Uttar Pradesh, Delhi, Manipur, Maharashtra, Chhattisgarh, Jammu and Kashmir, Goa and Haryana, for example, but also within the regions themselves.

Large concentrations of certain names are found within particular regions – but, it should be stressed, not all are solely confined to only one region.

Karavadra, Lal, Patel and *Shah* are common in Gujarat, where the language is Gujarati.

Names such as *Baidya*, *Chatterjee* and *Gupta* are found in West Bengal, where the language is

Bengali, while in the Hindi-speaking regions of Bihar and Jharkhand commonly found names include *Akhauri*, *Dhanjit*, *Pathik*, *Singh* and *Sinha*.

In Orissa, where the language is Oriya, names such as *Patnaik*, *Hati*, *Raj*, *Guru*, *Padhi*, *Samantray* and, again, *Singh*, predominate, while in the Telugu-speaking region of Andhra Pradesh common last names include *Adhikaria*, *Badam*, *Chowdary*, *Dasari*, *Godavarthi*, *Naidu*, *Setty* and *Varma*.

In the areas of Himachal Pradesh, Rajasthan, Uttarakhand, Uttar Pradesh and Delhi, where a number of different languages are spoken, popular names include *Agrawal*, *Bhati*, *Chand*, *Chaudhary*, *Dhowi*, *Khatri*, *Mathur*, *Panwar*, *Rana*, *Shahalia*, *Verma* and *Vajpai*.

In the Manipuri-speaking region of Manipur, frequently found names include those of *Yumnan*, *Konsam*, *Sewram*, *Chakpram*, *Kam* and *Oinam*, while in the Marathi-speaking area of Maharashtra commonly found names include *Mojad*, *Sarud*, *Soman*, *Pandit*, *Rasam* and *Sutar*.

In Chhattisgarh, where the languages spoken are Hindi and Chattisgarhi, names include *Agharia*, *Bhoi*, *Chandrakar*, *Nishad* and *Sahu*, while in Jammu and Kashmir, where the languages are

Kashmiri and Dogri, frequently found names include those of *Bhat*, *Maam*, *Rajwal*, *Sahgal*, *Samyal*, *Sharma* and *Tiku*.

Those found in Goa, where the languages are both Konkani and Marathi, include *Khandeparkar*, *Mendes*, *Parikar*, *Prabhu* and *Vernekar*, while in the Hindi and Haryanvi-speaking region of Haryana, common names include *Ahlawat*, *Beniwal*, *Dahiya*, *Saini* and *Talwar*.

Over the centuries many diverse factors have influenced the choice and the development of Indian family names – the key ones being not only those of language, or dialect, but those of ancestral birthplace, occupation, caste and religion.

In the majority of cases, but by no means exclusively, children are given three names – those of a 'given' one that roughly corresponds to the convention in the West of giving a child a 'Christian' forename, a second name, and a family, or third, one.

In some areas, where family names are not used, the third name may take the form of a revered religious figure or that of a grandfather or grandmother.

For those Hindus who belong to the upper

castes, their ancestry is indicated through what is known as his or her *gotra* – normally the name of an ancestor on the father's side, although it could also indicate the name of the ancestral village or profession.

Also in Hindu names, the family name frequently denotes the particular caste or community of Hindus to which the person belongs.

It is also common for Hindu families to hold a special name-giving ceremony shortly after a child's birth – after a horoscope of the child has been drawn up.

Adding further colour to the Hindu naming process is that many young children are also bestowed with a nickname – one chosen by either a family member or a close friend of the family.

In the religious community of the Sikhs, the majority of first names stem from ones derived from the classical language known as Sanskrit.

Sikh boys are also required to take the name of 'Singh' as a middle name, followed by a surname, or family name – while females of the faith are given the middle name of 'Kaur' or 'Gaur'.

Those Indians of the Jain faith frequently use 'Jain' as their last name, while many Jains of the

Gujarati region also use 'Shah' – derived from the Sanskrit word *sadhu*, denoting a monk.

Those Indians of the Muslim faith use Arabic names as their first, middle and last names.

Some, however, also use Indian names, particularly ones from the Urdu language – but only on strict condition that these names are not identified with any other religion.

The use of initials or abbreviations, rather than the full name, is very common with Indian names – the Punjabi cricketer Vikram Raj Vir Singh, more commonly known as V.R.V. Singh, being just one of many examples.

Adding to the rich variety of Indian names are those that derive from a particular occupation or profession.

One notable example is that of the great Indian social reformer, moral teacher and patriot Mohandas Karamchand Gandhi, better known to posterity as Mahatma Gandhi – whose family belonged to the caste of 'Gandhis', or 'grocers'.

The surnames of many Parsis, meanwhile, often end with 'wala', or 'wallah', indicating their line of work – such as 'Cyclewala', denoting a seller of bicycles.

Even more colourfully in recent years has been the practice of some Indians to adopt as their surname the English word for a particular profession – such as 'Engineer' – while, as in the West, it is also increasingly common to name children after famous celebrities such as film and sports stars.

But what all bearers of names have – be they of Indian, English, Scottish, Irish, Welsh or any other roots, and no matter where they are settled – is an ancient and indissoluble link with the country in which the name originated, making them heirs to its proud heritage and traditions.

Chapter two:

Freedom at midnight

Of truly ancient roots dating back to at least 4000 B.C., 'Khan' is a Muslim surname and also a title of Mongolian origin.

Derived from 'Khagan', denoting 'chief', or 'ruler', it was bestowed on the historical figure we know today as Genghis Khan, the founder of the mighty Mongolian Empire.

Known as 'Great Khan, or 'Emperor' and born in 1162 in modern-day northern Mongolia near its capital of Ulaanbaatar, his birth name 'Temujin' denoted 'blacksmith.'

He died in 1227, some sources asserting killed in battle, while his equally warlike descendants went on to expand the empire he had created by invading and conquering vast swathes of modern-day nations and territories that include China, Central Asia, Southwest Asia, the Caucasus, Russia and Eastern Europe.

The Khan name today, although its bearers are particularly identified with present-day Pakistan and Bangladesh, is found worldwide.

In the United Kingdom it is ranked 80th in some lists of the 100 most common surnames, while a survey carried out in 2014 showed that it is the most common Asian surname among doctors practising in Britain.

But it is on the Indian subcontinent that the name first enters the historical record, with many of its bearers witness to the most pivotal event in the history of the Indian subcontinent.

This was the bitter bloody struggle for independence that led in 1947 to the partition of India and Pakistan and the creation of the independent nations of India, Pakistan and, later, Bangladesh.

Resistance to British rule in India had stretched as far back as 1853, when Indian landholders in Bengal first mooted the idea of self-rule.

Just over 100 years before this, however, British public opinion was outraged at what became known as the horror of "The Black Hole of Calcutta".

It June of 1756 Siraj ud-Daulah, Nawab of Bengal, in reaction to the increasing meddling in the affairs of his province by the East India Company, captured its stronghold of Fort William, in Calcutta.

Up to 146 European civilians and British and Anglo-Indian soldiers were thrown into the cramped and fetid confines of a small dungeon in the fort and, according to the subsequent testimony of one of the soldiers, John Holwell, he was one of only 23 who survived the ordeal.

But Holwell's claims, following a number of detailed investigations over the years, now appear to have been greatly exaggerated, although it is beyond doubt that an incident of some horrific nature did indeed occur.

The nation was drenched in blood during the Indian Mutiny of 1857 to 1858. This uprising was sparked off when sepoys – as Indian soldiers serving in the army were known – revolted over a rumour that rifle bullets were greased by pig fat, considered unclean and therefore abhorrent to the Hindu faith.

Horror tales of atrocities against Europeans provoked outrage in Britain and the mutiny was brutally suppressed.

But although the rebellion was quelled, the widespread disquiet of the native Indians grew, and an Indian Association to push for a range of reforms was created in 1876.

Reforms were introduced in 1884 and for the first time native Indian judges could try Europeans for misdemeanours.

The resultant objections to this from Anglo-Indian interests further fuelled native anger leading to the creation in Bombay a year later of the Indian National Congress, the first independence movement in the British Empire in Asia and Africa.

The reforming Indian Councils Act was passed seven years later.

This granted more power to locally elected provincial councils, but the benefits of this paled into insignificance when, at the same time, Britain imposed a crippling duty on cotton imported from India.

In 1906, the Muslim League was formed in opposition to what was perceived as rising Hindu influence in the push for reform, while Mahatma Gandhi – a lawyer who had spent some time in South Africa – headed a campaign of passive resistance against British rule.

In 1919, meanwhile, even the British authorities themselves were shocked when nearly 380 unarmed civilians who had gathered for a protest meeting at Amritsar, in the Punjab, were shot and killed by a squad of Gurkhas commanded by General Reginal Dyer.

Events moved swiftly, with Jawaharlal Nehru, Subhas Chandra Bose and the Muslim League leader Muhammad Ali Jinnah taking centre stage with Gandhi in what became known as the 'Quit India' campaign.

It was not until midnight on the 14/15 August of 1947, overseen by the last British viceroy of India, Lord Mountbatten, that India was finally granted its independence – with the nation partitioned to form the new Muslim state of Pakistan.

But this came at great cost to life – with up to 250,000 people massacred as nearly 5.5million Hindus and Muslims such as the Khans were compelled to migrate to either the newly-created nation state of India or the predominantly Muslim state of Pakistan – while the new nation of Bangladesh, formerly East Pakistan, was created in 1971.

Gandhi, who had striven for Hindu-Muslim unity, was killed by a deranged Hindu assassin on January 30, 1948, while Muhammad Ali Jinnah, who became the first Governor-General of Pakistan, died later the same year.

In 1951, Jawaharlal Nehru won the first elections for the India Congress Party.

Born in 1907 in Rohana, a small village in the Hazara district of what was then the North-West Frontier Province of British India, Muhammad Ayub

Khan, better known as Ayub Khan, was the soldier who rose to become the second President of Pakistan.

Trained at the British military academy at Sandhurst and fighting in the British Indian Army during the Second World War, after independence he was appointed chief military commander for East Bengal and, in 1951, Commander-in-Chief of the Pakistan Army.

Following a bloodless coup in 1958 against President Iskander Mirza, he became the nation's second president, serving in the post until forced to resign five years before his death in 1974 because of a popular uprising against his rule.

Born in 1907 in the village of Balai in Dhamrai, in the Dhaka district, Ataur Rahman Khan, who had joined the Muslim League in 1944, served as Prime Minister of Bangladesh from March of 1984 until January of the following year; he died in 1991.

Chapter three:

Honours and distinction

Bearers of the proud name of Khan have gained distinction on the bloody field of battle.

During the First World War, Khudadad Khan was a recipient of the Victoria Cross (VC), the highest award for gallantry in the face of enemy action for British and Commonwealth forces.

Born in 1888 in the village of Dab in Chakwal district in what was then Punjab Province, British India – now in Pakistan – he had been serving as a sepoy in the 129th Duke of Connaught's Own Baluchis, British Indian Army, on the Western Front.

In October of 1914, during the First Battle of Ypres, he and his fellow Baluchis kept up a determined resistance against a German attack near the village of Gheluvelt, in Belgium, despite being heavily outnumbered.

His machine-gun unit kept the enemy at bay until finally overwhelmed, with Khan still firing his weapon as his comrades lay dead around him.

Badly wounded, he was left for dead and the

award of the VC was in recognition of him and his team having held up the Germans long enough for reinforcements to arrive and strengthen the line.

He died in 1971, while his VC is now on display at his ancestral home in Dab and there is a statue to him at the entrance to the Pakistan Army Museum in Rawalpindi.

Another particularly heroic bearer of the Khan name was Nor-un-Inayat Khan, who operated for the Allies during the Second World War in the highly dangerous role of a secret agent in Occupied France.

Better known as Inayat Khan, she was born in 1914 in St Petersburg to an Indian father and an Indian-American mother who was a descendant of Tipu Sultan, an eighteenth century ruler of the Mysore Kingdom.

The family moved to London shortly before the outbreak of the First World War and, in 1920, to Paris – fleeing back to Britain when France was overrun by the Germans in the summer of 1940.

Her language skills and knowledge of France led to her being recruited by SOE (Special Operations Executive) that had been tasked by Winston Churchill to 'set Europe ablaze.'

Trained as a wireless operator and at times known variously as 'Madeleine', 'Jeanne-Marie Rennier' and 'Nora Baker', she was landed clandestinely in France in late 1943 by a Lysander aircraft and teamed up with the French Resistance network known as *Physician*.

The first female agent to be sent from Britain to France, and operating from Paris, she was betrayed to the Germans by a double agent on October 13, 1943 and captured and imprisoned by the SD (Sicherheitsdienst), the intelligence agency of the SS and the Nazi Party.

Held in the feared SD headquarters at 84 Foch Avenue, she and two fellow SOE agents who had also been rounded up, managed to escape on November 25 – but were quickly recaptured.

She was eventually taken to the hell of Dachau concentration camp where, on September 11, 1944 she and three other female agents – Madeleine Damerment, Yolande Beekman and Eliane Plewman – were executed by a shot to the back of the head.

Posthumously awarded the George Cross, Britain's highest civilian honour, and the French Croix de Guerre with Silver Star, memorials to her include a bronze bust in Gordon Square Gardens, London, unveiled by the Princess Royal in 2012.

She was also commemorated in 2014 through the issue by the Royal Mail of its "Remarkable Lives" set of stamps.

Not only Pakistan's most famous cricketer but also a politician and philanthropist, Imran Khan Niazi, better known as Imran Khan, was born in 1952 in Lahore, Punjab.

Playing for his country between 1971 and 1992, he captained the Pakistan cricket team that won the Cricket World Cup in 1992.

Named *Wisden* Cricketer of the Year in 1983, he was inducted into the ICC (International Cricket Council) Hall of Fame in 2010.

As a politician, he was the founder in 1996 of the political party Tehreek-e-Insaf (Movement for Justice), while as a philanthropist his many initiatives include the founding of the Shaukat Khanum Memorial Cancer Hospital and the Namal College, Mianwali.

Married from 1995 to 2004 to Jemima Goldsmith, daughter of the wealthy financier Sir James Goldsmith, he married the British-Pakistani journalist Reham Khan in 2005.

The recipient of an honorary fellowship by the Royal College of Physicians of Edinburgh in recognition of his services for cancer treatment in Pakistan, in 2012 he was selected as the Asia Society's Person of the Year.

One of a famous dynasty of Khans, Sir Sikandar Hayat-Khan, born in 1892, was the Indian soldier, politician and statesman who was a prominent figure in the Unionist Muslim League.

One of the first Indian officers to receive the King's Commission, he served with distinction during the First World War with the 2/67th Punjabis and, also having fought in the Third Afghan War of May of 1919 to August of that year, was made an MBE by what was then the government of British India, and later received a knighthood.

Having served as Prime Minister of Punjab from 1937 until his death in 1942, one of his daughters, Tahira Mazhar Ali Khan, was a prominent campaigner for women's rights in Pakistan.

Born in 1924, she was married to the Pakistani journalist and socialist intellectual Mazhar Ali Khan. They were the parents of the British-Pakistani journalist, writer and former political activist Tariq Ali.

Born in Lahore in 1943, his early activism against Pakistan's military dictatorship led to him following the advice of an uncle, who worked in military intelligence that, for his own safety, he should leave the country.

Settling in Britain, he studied at Exeter College, Oxford and was elected president of the Oxford Union in 1965.

A prominent figure in the New Left movement that arose in the 1960s and a leading campaigner against the Vietnam War and a former member of the International Marxist Group (IMG), he is also a prolific author.

A contributor to a range of publications that include *New Left Review* and the *Guardian*, his many books include the 1970 *Pakistan: Military Rule or People's Power*, the 2003 *Bush in Babylon* and the 2015 *The Extreme Centre: A Warning*.

In contemporary politics Sadiq Khan is the Labour Party politician born into a working class British-Pakistani family in Tooting, London in 1970.

Working as a solicitor specialising in human rights, he served as a Labour councillor for the London borough of Wandsworth before being elected MP for Tooting in 2005.

Having held a number of government posts including Minister of State for Communities and Minister of State for Transport and Shadow Cabinet positions including Secretary of State for Justice, he resigned as an MP in 2016 after being elected Mayor of London.

In this role he has championed a number of initiatives including a dramatic reduction in the number of polluting vehicles in Central London and mutual tolerance among the city's varied communities.

Chapter four:
On the world stage

The proud name of Khan features prominently at an international level through a colourful range of endeavours and pursuits, in particular as stars of the silver screen and in music and sport.

India is famed for the Hindi language cinema industry known as 'Bollywood', a term originally coined for epics made in the bustling city of Mumbai, but now a term for the Indian film industry in general.

A star of Bollywood and Hollywood, **Irrfan Khan** was the actor born in 1967 in Jaipur, Rajasthan.

Considered one of India's finest actors, his performance in *Paan Singh Tomar* won him the 2012 Indian National Film Award for Best Actor.

Also the winner of the 2014 Asian Film Award for Best Actor and a recipient of the Padma Shri – India's fourth highest civilian honour – for his contribution to the arts, his Hollywood credits include the 2012 *Life of Pi*, the 2015 *Jurassic World* and, from 2006, the film adaptation of the best-selling Dan Brown novel *Inferno*, starring Tom Hanks; he died in 2020.

In Bollywood, **Salim Khan** is a member of a famed Indian acting dynasty.

Born in 1935 in Indore, in the modern day state of Maydha Pradesh, the actor and screenwriter has been married twice – to Sushila Charak, known as **Salma Khan** and the actress and dancer Helen Richardson, who is credited simply as **Helen**.

Born in 1938 in Burma to an Anglo-Indian father and a Burmese mother, she has collaborated with her husband on a number of films that include the 1971 *Adhikar*, the 1973 *Zanjeer* and, from 1987, *Mr India*.

Through his first marriage to Salma Khan, Salim Khan is the father of the leading Bollywood actors, Arbaaz, Salman and Sohail Khan.

Born in Pune in 1967, **Arbaaz Khan** is the award-winning actor, director and producer whose company Arbaaz Khan Productions was behind the 2010 film *Dabangg*.

One of the highest box office-grossing Bollywood films of all time, it won Khan the National Film Award for Best Popular Film Providing Wholesome Entertainment.

As an actor, his credits include the 1996 *Daraar*, for which he received the Filmfare Best

Villain Award, the 1998 *Pyaar Kiya To Darna Kya* and, from 2004, *Garv: Pride and Honour*.

Starring in *Dabangg* was his older brother **Salman Khan**.

Born in 1965, ranked as India's highest earning actor and also the second "most Googled Indian of 2015", his many film credits include the 1998 *Kuch Kuch Hoto Hai*, for which he was awarded the Filmfare Award for Best Supporting Actor, the 2011 *Bodyguard* and, from 2015, *Prem Ratan Dhan Payo*.

His brother **Sohail Khan**, born in 1969, is the actor, director and producer whose directing credits include the 1997 thriller *Auzaar*.

Known as a style icon, **Feroz Khan** was the actor, director, producer and film editor born in Bangalore in 1939.

Renowned for his distinctive swagger and trademark cigar and a star of films throughout the 1960s, 70s, and 80s, that include the 1980 *Qurbani*, and honoured with a Filmfare Lifetime Achievement Award – he died in 2009.

Recipient of the Filmfare Best Debut Award for his role in the 1998 *Prem Aggan*, **Fardeen Khan**, born in 1974, is the Bollywood actor whose other screen credits include the 2002 *Boot*, the 2005 *No Entry* and, from 2009, *All the Best Fun Begins*.

Known as "Bardash of Bollywood", or "King Bollywood" and "King Khan", Ahahrukh Khan, better known as **Shah Rukh Khan** or **SRK**, is the actor and producer whose many honours include fourteen Filmfare Awards.

With screen credits that include the 1992 *Deewana*, the 2002 *Devolas* and the 2010 *My Name is Khan*, he was the recipient in 2011 of the UNESCO Pyramide con Marni Award for his work in supporting children's education.

Rated as one of the world's most successful film stars in terms of box-office appeal and income, he was named by *Newsweek* magazine in 2008 as one of its fifty most powerful people in the world.

Born in Mumbai in 1965, **Aamir Khan** is the actor, director and producer whose many acting credits include the 1989 *Raakh*, for which he won a Special Jury Award at the National Film Awards, the 1996 *Raja Hindustan*, for which he won a Filmfare Award for Best Actor and the 1998 Indian-Canadian production *Earth*.

Director of films that include the 2014 *PK* – one of Bollywood's highest grossing films – and a recipient in 2003 of the Padma Shri and in 2010 the Padma Bushan, India's third highest civilian award, he is the uncle of the American-Indian actor **Imran Khan**.

Born in 1983 in Madison, Wisconsin of Indian roots, his screen credits include the 2011 *Delhi Belly*.

Recipient of the National Film Award for Best Actor for his role in the 2004 *Hum Tum*, **Saif Ali Khan** is the actor and producer born in 1970 in New Delhi.

On British shores and in the world of dance, **Akram Hossain Khan** is the dancer and choreographer of Bangladeshi descent born in London in 1974.

Trained from an early age in the South Asian dance genre known as Kathak and also in contemporary dance, he was aged thirteen when he was cast in theatre and film director Peter Brook's Shakespeare Company production of the Indian epic *Mahabharata*.

In collaboration with Nitin Sawhney and Anish Kapoor, he performed his work *Kaash* at the 2002 Edinburgh Festival, while he has also served as choreographer-in-residence at the Southbank Centre, London.

Choreographer for a section of Australian

singer Kyle Minogue's 2006 *Showgirl Concert* and also performing at the opening ceremony of the 2012 London Olympics, he is the recipient of an MBE for his services to dance.

On the television screen, **Tasmin Lucia-Khan**, born in London in 1980 of Bangladeshi descent, is the news presenter and anchor who has worked for BBC Three News and ITN's *Daybreak* in addition to other channels including BBC Asian Network.

Nominated for the 2008 Young Achiever Awards at the Asian Women Awards for Excellence, she was named by the British weekly newspaper *Eastern Eye* in 2010 as "27th sexiest Asian woman in the world".

In music, Yvette Marie Stevens is the American singer and songwriter who changed her name after she married to **Chaka Khan**.

Born in Chicago in 1953, it was with the funk band Rufus that she first came to prominence with the 1973 album *Talking Book*.

Hits enjoyed by the band have included *Once You Get Started*, *Sweet Thing* and *Midnight (My Love Will Lift You Up)*, while Khan enjoyed international success with her 1978 solo single *I'm Every Woman*.

Known as the Queen of Funk, she has been inducted twice into the Rock and Roll Hall of Fame – as a member of Rufus and as a solo artist.

The stepdaughter of the actress and singer Salma Agha and half-sister of the actress Sasha Agha, **Natasha Khan**, better known by her stage name of **Bat for Lashes**, is the English singer and songwriter whose 2006 album *Fur and Gold* and the 2009 *Two Suns* both received Mercury Prize nominations.

Born in 1979 in London to a Pakistani father and an Indian mother, she is also the vocalist for the band Sexwitch.

Bearers of the Khan name have also excelled in the highly competitive world of sport.

In the boxing ring, **Amir Khan** was aged seventeen when he won a silver medal as a lightweight at the 2004 Olympics – making him Britain's youngest Olympic boxing medallist.

Born in 1986 in Bolton, Greater Manchester, of roots in Pakistan's Rawalpindi district of the Punjab, he started competing competitively when he was aged 11.

Having turned professional in 2005, in 2009, after having moved up to the light-welterweight division, he secured his first WBA (World Boxing

Association) championship title when he defeated Andreas Kotelnik.

Also having held the unified WBA and IBF (International Boxing Federation) championship titles, he has also held the WBC (World Boxing Council) Silver Welterweight title.

He is the older brother of **Haroon "Harry" Khan**, the English retired professional boxer born in Bolton in 1991; opting to represent Pakistan at the 2010 Commonwealth Games, he won the bronze medal in the super flyweight division.

He and his brother Amir are cousins of **Sajid Mahmood**, born in Bolton in 1981, and who has played for England at county cricket level for Essex.

Also on the cricket pitch, Mansoor Ali Khan, also known as Mansur Ali Khan and as M.A.K. Pataudi, was the player described as "India's greatest cricket captain".

Nicknamed "Tiger Pataudi" and born in Bhopal in 1941, he was appointed captain of his national team in 1962 and played 46 Test matches between 1961 and 1975 – scoring an impressive total of 2,793 runs.

Also having played in England for Oxford

and Sussex, *Wisden* Cricketer of the Year in 1968 and manager of the India cricket team in 1974-75, he died in 2011 – while through his marriage to the actress Sharmila Tagore he was the father of the actor and producer Saif Khan, referred to earlier in this chapter.

Born in 1962 in Dhaka, **Athar Khan** is the Bangladeshi former middle order batsman who throughout his career played 19 ODI's (One Day Internationals) for his nation, and who has been a national team selector.

On the golf course, **Simon Khan**, born in 1972 in Chingford, is the English professional who secured a European Tour win at the Celtic Manor Wales Open in 2004.

On the squash court, **Jahangir Khan**, considered the greatest player in the history of the sport, was born in Karachi in 1963.

Unbeaten in competitive play from 1981 to 1986, he won the World Open six times and the British Open ten times.

Retiring from the game in 1993, he served from 2002 to 2008 as president of the World Squash federation.

Also on the squash court, **Jansher Khan**, born in 1969 in Peshawar, Pakistan, is the former professional player nicknamed "King Khan" and "The Punisher."

Winner of the World Open eight times and the British Open six times, he was the World Number 1 in the sport for more than ten years.

One cerebrally accomplished bearer of the proud name of Khan was **Alik Mir Sultan Khan**, a top world chess player of the 1930s and recognised as "perhaps the greatest natural player of modern times."

Born of humble origins in 1905 in what was then United Punjab, British India, he was aged nine when his father taught him Indian chess.

Winner of the All-India Championship in 1928, he came to international attention in 1928 when, as a servant to the Punjabi soldier and landowner Umar Hayat Khan, he travelled to Britain for an extended stay.

While there, he won the British Championship three times – in 1929, 1932 and 1933.

He died in his homeland in 1966 while, despite his mastery of the game and for reasons best known to itself, the World Chess Federation never awarded him any titles, such as Grandmaster or International Master.